MW01133888

Pebble™

Helpers in Our Community

We Need Plumbers

by Helen Frost

Consulting Editor: Gail Saunders-Smith, PhD
Consultant: Larry Oliver, President
The American Society of Plumbing Engineers
Chicago, Illinois

Capstone
press

Mankato, Minnesota

Pebble Books are published by Capstone Press
151 Good Counsel Drive, P.O. Box 669, Mankato, Minnesota 56002
www.capstonepress.com

1 2 3 4 5 6 09 08 07 06 05 04

Library of Congress Cataloging-in-Publication Data
Frost, Helen, 1949–
    We need plumbers / by Helen Frost.
        p. cm.—(Helpers in our community)
    Includes bibliographical references and index.
    ISBN 0-7368-2576-2 (hardcover)
    1. Plumbing—Vocational guidance—Juvenile literature. 2. Plumbers—Juvenile
literature. [1. Plumbers. 2. Occupations.] I. Title. II. Series.
TH6124.F77 2005
696'.1'023—dc22   2003024242

Summary: Simple text and photographs describe and illustrate plumbers.

Note to Parents and Teachers

The Helpers in Our Community series supports national social studies standards related to community helpers and their roles. This book describes and illustrates plumbers. The photographs support early readers in understanding the text. The repetition of words and phrases helps early readers learn new words. This book also introduces early readers to subject-specific vocabulary words, which are defined in the Glossary. Early readers may need assistance to read some words and to use the Table of Contents, Glossary, Read More, Internet Sites, and Index/Word List sections of the book.

Table of Contents

What Plumbers Do

Plumbers put pipes in buildings and under the ground. Water flows through pipes.

Clean water goes into buildings through pipes. Dirty water flows out of buildings through other pipes.

8

Plumbers put pipes together.
They use pipes of many
shapes and sizes.

Plumbers put sinks, toilets, and bathtubs in buildings. They connect them to pipes.

Plumbers fix pipes
that leak. They
replace broken pipes.

Tools Plumbers Use

Plumbers use wrenches to loosen and tighten fittings. Fittings connect pipes.

Plumbers cut pipes.
They use a tool called
a pipe cutter.

Plumbers clean pipes and drains. They use a tool called a snake.

We Need Plumbers

Plumbers help keep water flowing into and out of buildings.

Glossary

fitting—a small metal or plastic connector between pipes

pipe—a tube; pipes usually carry liquid or gas; pipes are made of metal, plastic, or glass.

snake—a long metal coil; snakes can bend to fit in different pipes; plumbers put snakes into pipes to get rid of clogs.

wrench—a tool with grips to tighten and loosen fittings, nuts, and other items

Read More

Simon, Charnan. *Plumbers.* Wonder Books. Chanhassen, Minn.: Child's World, 2003.

Thomas, Mark. *A Day with a Plumber.* Hard Work. New York: Children's Press, 2001.

Internet Sites

FactHound offers a safe, fun way to find Internet sites related to this book. All of the sites on FactHound have been researched by our staff.

Here's how:

1. Visit *www.facthound.com*
2. Type in this special code **0736825762** for age-appropriate sites. Or enter a search word related to this book for a more general search.
3. Click on the **Fetch It** button.

FactHound will fetch the best sites for you!

Index/Word List

bathtubs, 11
broken, 13
buildings, 5,
  7, 11, 21
clean, 7, 19
connect,
  11, 15

cut, 17
dirty, 7
drains, 19
fittings, 15
fix, 13
leak, 13
pipe cutter, 17

replace, 13
sinks, 11
snake, 19
toilets, 11
tools, 17, 19
water, 5,
  7, 21

Word Count: 107
Early-Intervention Level: 13

Editorial Credits
Mari C. Schuh, editor; Abby Bradford, Bradford Design Inc., cover designer;
  Enoch Peterson, book designer; Wanda Winch, photo researcher; Karen Hieb,
  product planning editor

Photo Credits
Corbis/Jon Feingersh, 20
Folio, Inc./Mark E. Gibson, cover
Index Stock Imagery/Omni Photo Communications Inc., 6
Laura N. Scott Imagery, 1, 8, 12, 16, 18
Photri-Microstock/J. D. Barnell, 14
Unicorn Stock Photos/D & I MacDonald, 4; Jeff Greenberg, 10

The author thanks the children's library staff at the Allen County Public Library in
Fort Wayne, Indiana, for research assistance.